SELF CARE FOR STUDENTS

Simple Well-Being Tips to Help You Survive University

FRANKIE YOUNG

vie

SELF-CARE FOR STUDENTS

Text by Amanda Marples

An Hachette UK Company
www.hachette.co.uk

Vie Books, an imprint of Summersdale Publishers Ltd
Part of Octopus Publishing Group Limited
Carmelite House
50 Victoria Embankment
LONDON
EC4Y 0DZ
UK

www.summersdale.com

Printed and bound in Poland

ISBN: 978-1-83799-143-3

Substantial discounts on bulk quantities of Summersdale books are available to corporations, professional associations and other organizations. For details contact general enquiries: telephone: +44 (0) 1243 771107 or email: enquiries@summersdale.com.

INTRODUCTION

Self-care can feel like yet another urgent, time-consuming chore to complete, especially if you are a student. It might feel like a luxury you can't afford, but it needn't be complicated. Self-care doesn't require expensive vitamins, boundless energy or long stretches of time, and it isn't about doing it perfectly or expecting all your worries to dissolve away. In this book you will find simple tips and ideas to help reduce stress, foster well-being and allow you to thrive while in higher education. Well done for being here. It's time to take good care of yourself.

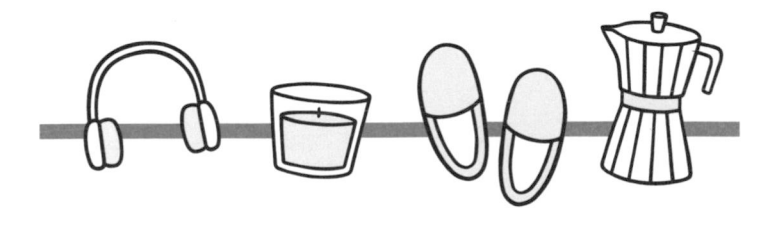

I HAVE COME
TO BELIEVE THAT
CARING FOR
MYSELF IS NOT
SELF-INDULGENT.
CARING FOR
MYSELF IS AN
ACT OF SURVIVAL.

AUDRE LORDE

THE BENEFITS OF SELF-CARE

Effective self-care can help you...

★ Remain alert, focused and organized (and hand that assignment in on time)

★ Stay calm (and cope with exams)

★ Eat better (and spend less money on junk food)

★ Have energy (and actually make it to the concert/night out/society event)

★ Stabilize your mood (and cope with housemates)

★ Feel in control (and not overwhelmed when all your coursework is due at once)

★ Sleep better (and wake with time to eat breakfast before lectures)

Does that all sound good? Read on for tips on how you can achieve this.

We can climb mountains with self-love.

Samira Wiley

It doesn't have to be difficult

Self-care can be hard work – and you've already got enough to deal with! Assignments, seminar prep, paid work, not to mention the overflowing laundry basket and the fact that you're out of milk. Yoga is hardly your top priority, right?

Go easy on yourself. Self-care is not just about downward-facing dogs. Maybe something quick such as spending 10 minutes at the end of the day hanging up your clothes might give you a better sense of balance. Self-care does require a little effort, so choose simple tasks that make you feel calmer.

I AM

DESERVING

OF THE BEST
POSSIBLE

CARE

CHANGE CAN BE TOUGH

If you are living away from home for the first time, you're probably feeling a little wobbly as well as excited. Self-care can be an anchor to help you feel steadier. What made you feel safe back home? What were your routines? A warm drink and a book at bedtime? Sitting down to eat with others? Fresh air every day? Catching up on your favourite TV show? Make a list of your home comforts and choose to introduce one activity you enjoyed at home every day while you explore your new independence.

LEAVING HOME
IN A SENSE
INVOLVES A
KIND OF SECOND
BIRTH IN WHICH
WE GIVE BIRTH
TO OURSELVES.

Robert Neelly Bellah

ALL CHANGE IS
HARD AT FIRST,
MESSY IN THE
MIDDLE AND
SO GORGEOUS
AT THE END.

ROBIN SHARMA

ADJUSTING TO CHANGE

Change can be stressful and starting university or college is no exception. Often it means moving to a new city or even a new country. It might involve making the transition from full-time employment to full-time studying, a reduced income or a different role.

Whatever your circumstances, give yourself time to adjust. You might at times feel weepy, anxious or worried that you've made a mistake. This is all normal, so try not to compare yourself with others, especially if they seem to be coping – everyone will be feeling doubts to some degree, no matter how well they hide it.

While you are adjusting, keep it simple. Eat breakfast, attend lectures (even if you don't feel like taking copious notes), change your clothes daily. Don't rush things, or yourself. Before long, you might find that you have carved out new routines, found your favourite place to sit in the library and learned how to work the washing machine. The unfamiliar will soon be the ordinary. Give yourself time.

I EMBRACE
CHANGE

The time to relax
is when you don't
have time for it.

Sydney J. Harris

TIREDNESS CAN GET IN THE WAY

Going to university or college means new and increased demands. Housemates to deal with, lecture theatres to find, public transport to navigate, not to mention a huge amount of incoming academic information to take on board. It's an intense time. You will be tired and self-care calls for effort that you might not feel ready to give.

Here is the irony: when you feel too tired for self-care, this is exactly when you need it the most. It is when you feel exhausted that you are likely to reach for unhealthy coping strategies that could make you feel bad later.

So, what can you do? Find compromises and pay attention to the small wins. Never enough time for breakfast in the morning? Get out a bowl and the packet of cereal the night before. Can't face 2 hours in the library? Commit to 45 minutes of that time studying at home. Too tired to make notes? Use voice notes instead or stick to reading the core text. You can always read more later.

It's okay. When you are tired, something is always better than nothing.

LONELINESS IS THE POVERTY OF SELF; SOLITUDE IS THE RICHNESS OF SELF.

May Sarton

NOT GOING OUT
IS TOTALLY FINE

Being a student is often associated with wild nights out. It can feel almost compulsory! But what if pubs and clubs are not your thing, or some nights you're tired and don't feel like it? Staying in might feel like you're not making the most of student life. Not true! Partying is only one way out of many to have fun. If you do want to experience the nightlife, be selective. Those evenings will likely feel more special if you do.

I AM

**STRONG,
COURAGEOUS**

AND

WHOLE

EVERYTHING
WILL BE OKAY
IN THE END.
IF IT'S NOT
OKAY, IT'S NOT
THE END.

JOHN LENNON

KEEP IT IN PERSPECTIVE

Sometimes we see the world in black and white. We tell ourselves we have to do something perfectly and consistently, or we are doing it wrong. This can make it hard for us to sustain good self-care habits and to see that doing a little of something is still a worthwhile, positive gain. Setting the bar too high, such as expecting yourself to go to the gym every single day, is setting yourself up for disappointment. When the inevitable day arrives when you don't feel like it, you are likely to see this as falling short, which can lead to giving up.

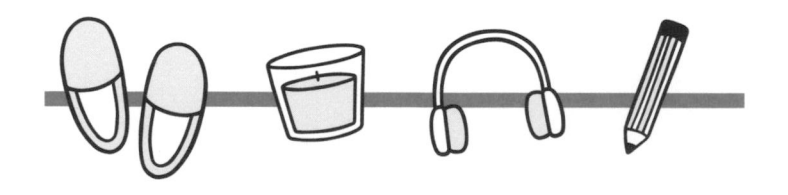

When you find yourself thinking in an all-or-nothing way, try to pause.

Keep things in perspective. Higher education is an amazing opportunity and it is natural to want to do as well as possible. But it isn't the be all and end all! Life is full of opportunity and plenty of very successful people struggled in higher education.

There is so much to gain from just being at university or college beyond academic success. Don't tell yourself you have to get a first-class degree or it's all for nothing – tell yourself it's enough to be here, doing it.

Nothing is impossible. The word itself says "I'm possible".

Audrey Hepburn

I USE
MY TIME
WISELY

What comes first?

Revise... start the project... go to the gym... run for student rep... call home...

Prioritizing is a tricky but essential skill. Without it you risk pushing yourself too hard, ignoring your well-being and burning out. When you feel overwhelmed, stop and breathe. Remember you cannot do everything. First, make a list. Next, listen to your body. Do you need to eat, shower, get some fresh air?

When you are ready, divide the list into two: time-pressured tasks, such as things with deadlines, and less essential chores that can wait. Set mini-deadlines for the urgent tasks and schedule everything else for tomorrow. Again: remember you cannot do everything.

SUCCESS
IS BUILT
SEQUENTIALLY.
IT'S ONE
THING AT
A TIME.

Gary W. Keller

WHATEVER YOU
FEAR MOST HAS
NO POWER.
IT IS YOUR
FEAR THAT HAS
THE POWER.

OPRAH WINFREY

WHO ARE YOU HERE FOR?

University or college can feel like a big responsibility. Perhaps you are the first in your family to get this far. Maybe you have a sponsor paying your fees. Perhaps you have a family of your own relying on you to succeed. Fear of letting others down can force you to overwork or avoid it completely. Don't let it. The people who matter will love you regardless of how well you do. Do your best, but do it for *you*.

I RELEASE
MY FEAR
OF
DISAPPOINTING
OTHERS

Self-care is not selfish. You cannot serve from an empty vessel.

Eleanor Brown

PUTTING YOU FIRST

If you don't rest enough, how can you expect to stay focused in the library? If you don't eat well, how can you expect to have enough energy to enjoy time spent with others? If you don't ask for help, how can you encourage others to do the same? If you don't look after yourself, how can you do your part of the project with confidence? Putting yourself first is not selfish; it is essential to your success as a student.

IF WE WERE
MEANT TO STAY
IN ONE PLACE,
WE'D HAVE
ROOTS INSTEAD
OF FEET.

Rachel Wolchin

A SENSE OF BELONGING

Starting university or college usually entails moving to a new town or city. To help you feel more connected to your new town... explore!

★ Recruit a housemate and take a bus to the other side of town, just for fun.

★ Use local newspapers to find out what's on in the city, not just the college or university publications.

★ Persuade a friend to take a trip to the countryside and enjoy a day out with you.

★ Learn the key landmarks to orient yourself – churches, shops, monuments.

★ Pin a map of the city to your wall.

I POSSESS ALL THE QUALITIES I NEED FOR SUCCESS

DEVELOPING A ROUTINE

Routines can help you feel grounded and safe, and provide a framework for self-care. But be cautious. Overplanning can make you feel overwhelmed. There's nothing more soul-destroying than devising the perfect routine that spans the whole day only to find you have wildly underestimated how long everything takes. If this happens to you, don't be discouraged. You can still build a routine, but start small and keep it simple.

Morning routines are a good place to start. Choose up to three initial activities for your morning: breakfast, a shower, perhaps some stretches. If you find you cannot consistently do all three, reduce it to two. Don't force it. When your routine has become second nature, you can consider adding in another task or activity. You don't need to fit all of your self-care practices into each day. Self-care is about being gentle with yourself and focusing on the things that really help you to feel balanced and well. Do likewise with your routine.

Physical health

Your body houses your mind. If you want to be able to solve complex problems, think critically, focus on dense academic texts or perform intricate analyses, the home your mind lives in – your body – needs to be nurtured. That means looking after your body by eating well, exercising, resting and attending to any problems that arise. Maintain your body carefully, listen to what it is telling you, take its needs seriously and you will be rewarded with a well-functioning mind.

PHYSICAL FITNESS IS THE FIRST REQUISITE OF HAPPINESS.

JOSEPH PILATES

MISSING HOME

Homesickness is normal. You may be living independently for the first time, and in a strange place. Here, self-care is about kindness and reassurance during this transitional period. The trick is to maintain just enough of a connection to home to enable you to feel safe yet confident enough to take steps forward into your new life. Having a regular time to call home is a good idea and it can also be reassuring to have a date in the calendar for a visit. If you don't now live too far away, you don't even have to wait until the end of term!

While homesickness usually passes, reach out for help if you are struggling. Your university or college will support you. Some students take leaves of absence on health or personal grounds, and sometimes it is possible to change courses to be nearer to home. No medals for bravery are awarded for forcing yourself to remain in an unhappy situation. If you are concerned, talk to your personal tutor or student counsellor to discuss what is right for you.

I long, as
does every human
being, to be at
home wherever
I find myself.

Maya Angelou

I HAVE

A RIGHT

TO BE

HERE

DO NOT FEEL LONELY, THE ENTIRE UNIVERSE IS INSIDE YOU.

Rumi

SAFETY ISN'T EXPENSIVE; IT'S PRICELESS.

JERRY SMITH

HAVE FUN, STAY SAFE

Self-care is not just about bubble baths and early nights. It's about making sensible decisions that put your safety first.

What does being sensible look like?

- ★ Never walking home alone at night
- ★ Telling a friend your whereabouts if you are meeting someone new
- ★ Teaming up with trusted friends on nights out
- ★ Never leaving your drink unattended or accepting a drink from a stranger

You could also find out if your student union offers free night buses or personal alarms.

Boring? Maybe. Important? Absolutely.

I TRUST
MY INTUITION

MAKING USE OF SUPPORT

Life never runs completely smoothly and when you're a student it's no different. If life is getting in the way of your studies – emotionally, financially or socially – your university or college will have ways to support you.

Most institutions will have...

★ Disabled student support

★ Mental health/counselling services

★ A student union offering free advice on finances, housing and academic matters

★ Student welfare services for times of crisis

Never be afraid to access support. These services exist for a reason!

True belonging doesn't require you to change who you are; it requires you to be who you are.

Brené Brown

FINDING YOUR PEOPLE

Feeling understood and accepted is crucial to well-being. This is especially true when you find yourself without your old friendship circle close by for immediate support. One way to take care of yourself is to find new communities to belong to.

This is particularly important if you have a disability, are neurodiverse, identify as LGBTQIA+ or are Black, Asian or from a minority ethnic background, since these are the people most likely to experience isolation and discrimination at some point in their lives. Specialized groups and societies exist in all institutions of higher education. Make it a priority to find out about them.

Regardless of your background, finding like-minded people to hang out with can help you feel safe, connected and comfortable to be who you are – whether you are passionate about conservation, love tap-dancing or are obsessed with *Stranger Things*.

Even if you are halfway through the year, it's never too late to join a group or society – most are always looking for new members, so why not head down to campus or check online and see what is available.

THERE IS NO
SUCH THING
AS TIME
MANAGEMENT;
THERE IS
ONLY SELF-
MANAGEMENT.

Rory Vaden

I HAVE

ALL THE TIME

I NEED TO

ACCOMPLISH

MY GOALS

PLANNING YOUR TIME

If you plan your time well, you will always have time for self-care. Sometimes in life it's okay to go with the flow and plan nothing at all. But being a student, it will be necessary to have a plan in one form or another to manage all your competing demands and deadlines.

A plan can help you to work consistently and reduce the possibility of overwhelm – especially if you are anxious about failure and prone to overworking or the opposite: avoidance. If you find yourself in these extremes, the need for self-care is more acute.

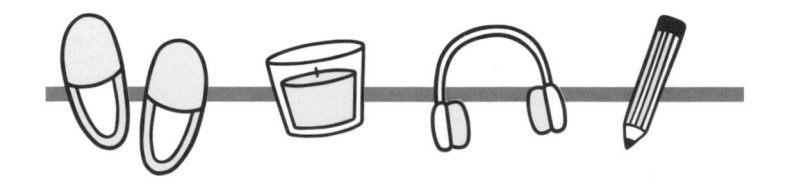

To better plan your time before overwhelm hits, the following might help you:

★ Build a timetable showing lectures, seminars, regular appointments and other commitments.

★ Decide on the parameters of your working day so you know when to stop.

★ Block out time for eating, rest and leisure.

★ Consider what time of day you are at your best and schedule your independent study for then.

★ Always make sure there are spaces where nothing is planned, to give your plan flexibility.

JUST BECAUSE
YOU MAKE A
GOOD PLAN,
DOESN'T MEAN
THAT'S WHAT'S
GONNA HAPPEN.

TAYLOR SWIFT

Success consists
of going from failure
to failure without
loss of enthusiasm.

David Guy Powers

PLANS ARE JUST INTENTIONS

A plan is necessary but should always be subject to change. Unforeseen events, cancelled lectures, illness or simply underestimating how long that reading will take can all throw you off course. When your plan falls to the wayside, don't panic. This is not failure. It's just life! With an attitude of curiosity, ask yourself what went wrong. Do you need to give yourself longer for seminar prep next week? Is the gym further away than you thought? Was it unrealistic to expect yourself to tidy your room after a day of lectures?

Be as flexible with your mindset as you are with your plan. Don't personalize it, just move on. You might have an all-or-nothing tendency to write off your carefully designed systems as soon as they go wrong, but try to resist this impulse. Don't abandon your plan – adjust it.

Remember to speak to yourself kindly: "Today didn't quite work out the way I intended. What can I do differently next time?"

MY PLANS ARE FLEXIBLE AND RESPONSIVE TO MY NEEDS

COOPERATION
IS ALWAYS MORE
POWERFUL THAN
COMPETITION.

Bob Proctor

SHARING SPACE

Living with anyone can be challenging and sharing student accommodation is no exception.

When you are sharing an apartment or a house, start as you mean to go on. Get to know your own boundaries:

★ How much noise can you tolerate?

★ Are you happy to be interrupted when in your room?

★ Do you want to socialize with the people you live with, or not?

★ How often are you willing to overlook someone using your shampoo?

★ Do you expect – or object – to house parties?

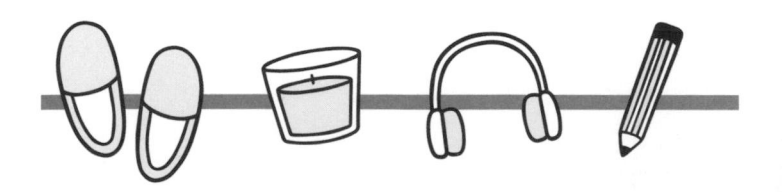

If you can, be clear about your boundaries from the outset and communicate them in a respectful way. Do not be afraid to repeat yourself. Rotas are very helpful for sharing domestic chores, as are assigning specific roles and responsibilities to each tenant. Some student apartments or houses accommodate as many as ten students, possibly more. Space will be at a premium, so an inviolable space of your own is an absolute must-have. Make your room your sanctuary.

THE IMPORTANCE
OF NUTRITION

The brain is the most energy-hungry organ in the body. If you want your brain to work optimally, it will need a regular intake of protein, carbohydrate and hydration.

Whether you are a die-hard consumer of red meat or a vegan, it is important to regularly check in with your diet. In a pressured higher education setting, it is so easy to eat for convenience and comfort. Try not to – or at least not every day.

Make shopping and cooking healthy meals part of your weekly plan. If your diet needs improvement, don't feel you must revolutionize it overnight. Perhaps start by eating three healthy meals a week, using fresh ingredients whenever you can. You might find you enjoy cooking from scratch instead of just grabbing something quick.

IT'S NOT ABOUT
EATING HEALTHY
TO LOSE WEIGHT.
IT'S ABOUT
EATING HEALTHY
TO FEEL GOOD.

DEMI LOVATO

When enough is enough

It can be hard to know when you have read enough, revised enough, written enough. Course or module handbooks may indicate how many hours of independent study is expected for each hour of teaching. Start there, but don't take it as set in stone. It is only a guide. Set your own daily parameters for starting and finishing your working day and try your best to stick to them. You might worry it isn't enough, but working until midnight will not help you to feel less worried!

I ALLOW MYSELF

AMPLE TIME

FOR

LEISURE

HOBBIES AND INTERESTS

"All work and no play makes Jack a dull boy," so the proverb goes. This is true. If all you ever do is study, you risk producing lacklustre work. The brain needs different kinds of stimulation to help it make connections to other areas of thinking. It's not uncommon for a difficult equation or concept to become suddenly crystal clear during a game of squash or while painting. Give your brain variety by pursuing your hobbies, or even finding yourself a new one through the clubs and societies on offer at your university or college. You never know, you might find you have a talent for archery or love for ballroom dancing you didn't know about.

Since there is nothing so well worth having as friends, never lose a chance to make them.

Francesco Guicciardini

MAKING FRIENDS

Making new friends can be daunting, but having people to hang out and share concerns with is essential to good mental health. Humans need other humans. If you feel anxious about this, get involved in some organized events. Most universities hold formal socials and taster sessions during the first weeks of term, so these can be a good place to start, as well as clubs and societies or joining your student union. Try to remember that most people feel anxious about meeting others at the start of their course, even if they hide it well!

YOUR BODY IS
YOUR TEMPLE.
YOU DO YOUR
BODY GOOD,
YOUR BODY
WILL DO
YOU GOOD.

Floyd Mayweather Jr

PERSONAL CARE

Self-care includes personal care. While we all have different thresholds, it's true that most of us feel better if we are clean and well groomed. It is just as important to take care of your body as it is to take care of your mind.

Here are some ideas:

★ A daily shower

★ Moisturizing

★ Styling your hair

★ Wearing clean, ironed clothes

★ Wearing cologne/aftershave

★ Regular haircuts

★ Clean nails

What aspects of personal care help you feel better about yourself? Choose your top three and schedule one thing today.

I TEND TO
MY BODY
AND
THE SPACE
IN WHICH
I LIVE

Time for chores

Looking after the space in which you live can help you feel calm and organized. If you find that the state of your living space is making you feel stressed, don't try to deal with it all at once. Think about what is bothering you the most. Making a start is always the hardest thing. Perhaps put on music or a podcast and set yourself a goal: "By the end of this track, I will have picked up all my clothes." You might even enjoy the time spent sorting and organizing your space, or at least feel better when it's done!

HAVE NOTHING
IN YOUR HOUSE
THAT YOU DO
NOT KNOW TO
BE USEFUL, OR
BELIEVE TO BE
BEAUTIFUL.

WILLIAM MORRIS

A budget is
telling your money
where to go instead
of wondering
where it went.

John C. Maxwell

FINANCES AND BUDGETING

Money is a concern for most students. You probably feel as if you never have enough. Setting a budget can be a reassuring act of self-care. After the essentials (rent, groceries, utilities), decide upon a budget for eating out, hobbies, movies – whatever gives you a sense of well-being. Giving yourself permission for these things can reduce impulse spending, take the guilt out of treating yourself and restore a sense of abundance. If you are not coping financially, don't wait until it's a crisis. Most universities and colleges offer emergency financial aid and advice, so ask for help early.

I HAVE A

HEALTHY

RELATIONSHIP
WITH

MONEY

IF YOU AVOID
CONFLICT TO
KEEP THE PEACE,
YOU START A
WAR INSIDE
YOURSELF.

Cheryl Richardson

WHEN CONFLICT ARISES

All relationships have their challenges, particularly when you live under the same roof. Problems between housemates are extremely common among students, ranging from minor irritations over whose turn it is to do the dishes to major conflicts over money or space.

If there is a conflict in your house, do...

★ Take time out to calm down – it is almost impossible to move forward from conflict otherwise.

★ Get an alternative view from family or friends – as long as they are not involved in the disagreement.

★ Think about what part you may have played in the conflict. Were you unfair? Unclear? Did you say or do the wrong thing?

★ If you cannot figure it out between yourselves, find out whether your accommodation or students' union offers mediation or advice on housemate disputes.

★ Be flexible and willing to compromise.

Do not...

★ Tackle a grievance when you are angry.

★ Tolerate physical or verbal abuse (or perpetrate it yourself).

★ Take sides in arguments that don't involve you.

★ Agree to things that are wrong or harmful for you, just to smooth things over.

★ Struggle alone.

REFUSE TO BE
DISHEARTENED,
DISCOURAGED,
DISTRACTED
FROM YOUR
GOALS IN LIFE.

BERNICE KING

I HAVE
CLARITY
AND
FOCUS

THE WORLD IS FULL OF DISTRACTIONS

Your life will be full of things that pull you away from the task at hand. Sometimes this is not a bad thing. Occasional diversions can be helpful, especially if you are approaching exhaustion.

But if you really need to focus, minimize distractions by...

★ Priming people – let your friends and family know that you are not available

★ Using free site-blocking software or apps

★ Turning off notifications and putting your phone on silent

★ Even better – putting your phone out of reach!

The moment
you put a deadline
on your dream,
it becomes a goal.

Harsha Bhogle

CONFIDENCE IS
KEY. SOMETIMES,
YOU NEED
TO LOOK
LIKE YOU'RE
CONFIDENT
EVEN WHEN
YOU'RE NOT.

Vanessa Hudgens

I AM

AT EASE

WHEN ASKED
TO GIVE

MY OPINION

CONTRIBUTING TO SEMINARS

Some students feel absolutely fine about speaking up in seminars or workshops. Other students find the prospect a little scary! Even if they don't make it obvious, many students feel highly anxious about being called on, getting it wrong or appearing foolish. This can lead to staying quiet or avoiding the seminar completely. Sometimes participation is compulsory and graded, but even if it is not, contributing to discussion will help with your confidence and enhance your learning.

If you find this aspect of academic life difficult, how can you make this easier on yourself?

★ Plan ideas, thoughts or questions in advance – is there something in the topic or text that is interesting to you?

★ Connect with your peers. Agree with opinions when appropriate and if someone else confesses to not understanding, confess along with them!

★ Don't be afraid to step out of the room if you need a minute to compose yourself.

★ Give yourself time before and after the session to breathe, be quiet, settle your mind or get reassurance from friends.

IT'S NOT ABOUT
FINDING YOUR
VOICE; IT'S ABOUT
GIVING YOURSELF
PERMISSION TO
USE YOUR VOICE.

KRIS CARR

There is hope, even when your brain tells you there isn't.

John Green

EXIT STRATEGIES

There's nothing wrong with bailing out. In fact, sometimes it's necessary. You might feel overwhelmed in large lecture halls or panicky in a crowded bar. Sometimes it is not about anxiety, but simply that your mind is telling you that you are ready to go home. Plan your exit in advance and reassure yourself that you are free to leave.

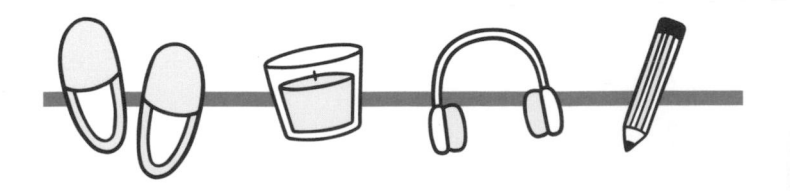

Here are some ideas:

★ Be strategic about where you sit in lectures, seminars or workshops. Sitting near the door can allow you to slip out discreetly if necessary.

★ Make academic staff aware in advance if you might have to leave early. Do likewise with friends if you are not sure about a night out.

★ Excusing yourself to use the bathroom is a great cover story if you need a quiet moment, and something that normally will not be questioned.

★ Prepare a simple statement such as: "It's getting late and I have lectures/work tomorrow."

★ Remember it is enough to say, "I have an appointment", even if that appointment is with yourself!

I DO
ONE THING
AT A TIME

YOU CAN'T CALM THE STORM, SO STOP TRYING. WHAT YOU CAN DO IS CALM YOURSELF. THE STORM WILL PASS.

Timber Hawkeye

DEALING WITH OVERWHELM

Everyone has a tipping point, a coping threshold. Your threshold can move up or down depending on your mental health, current level of demand and other vulnerabilities. Prevention is better than cure. Taking action before you reach that point will improve your sense of agency and resilience.

But no matter how diligent you are with your self-care, you may still be overwhelmed at times. Don't ignore the signs, which include forgetfulness, loss of focus, anxiety and irritability. If you are becoming overwhelmed, the most self-caring thing to do is...

STOP

If you find yourself in this situation, seek support from student counsellors, family or friends. It might be that all you need is a day or two off, or if that isn't enough, you may need to seek academic guidance from your personal tutor. You might need an extension or variation to your courses/ modules. There is no shame in needing extra support. You may be surprised how many students need this from time to time. Whatever you decide, pushing yourself harder is not the solution!

REMEMBER TO
BREATHE. IT IS,
AFTER ALL, THE
SECRET TO LIFE.

GREGORY MAGUIRE

TIME TO CHECK IN

When you meet with a friend, what's the first thing you say?

"HEY, HOW ARE YOU?"
"HOW ARE THINGS?"
"HOW'S IT GOING?"

Get in the habit of regularly asking yourself these questions.

"How am I physically? Emotionally? Mentally? Socially? Financially?"

If the answer is, "Not too great, actually..." ask yourself, do you need to...

★ Skip the night out?

★ See the doctor?

★ Drop a shift?

★ Watch the lecture recording instead of attending?

★ Go to yoga?

★ Call home?

★ Get advice on something?

Check in, answer honestly and take action.

I ALLOW
MYSELF TO
SLOW DOWN
AND
BREATHE

To prevent fatigue and worry, the first rule is: rest often. Rest before you get tired.

Dale Carnegie

THE IMPORTANCE OF REST

To function well, to be sharp, alert, creative and focused, you need regular and adequate rest. It is very difficult for your body to make up for a deficit. Try not to get in deficit. That means going to bed on time – or at least some of the time, even when you really want to watch the next episode. It means not working excessive hours. It means listening to your body when it aches, when it feels like you are wading through treacle. It means responding to those signs.

If you have difficulty sleeping, restful activity is a good second best. Why not try...

★ A warm bath or shower
★ Reading fiction (not *Super-Advanced Theories of Political Economy in Early Modern Civilizations!*)
★ Puzzles, such as crosswords or sudoku
★ Jigsaws
★ Gentle yoga or stretching
★ Crafts
★ Adult colouring books
★ Music (playing or listening)
★ Meditation

THROUGH SLEEP, YOU DISCONNECT FROM THE WORLD SO YOU CAN RECONNECT WITH YOUR SOUL.

Jennifer Williamson

SLEEP IS THAT
GOLDEN CHAIN
THAT TIES HEALTH
AND OUR BODIES
TOGETHER.

THOMAS DEKKER

SLEEP HYGIENE

Sleep is important to health, but is typically cited by students as an area of difficulty. Not all self-care feels pleasant. Sometimes it's boring, like eating your greens. The dos and don'ts of good sleep hygiene practices can feel a bit like that. But as with all of the advice in this book, just do what you can, as often as you can.

With that in mind, here are some tips for restful sleep...

★ Set a regular bedtime and waking time.

★ Avoid daytime napping.

★ Avoid caffeine, sugar or other stimulants after 2pm.

★ Avoid screens (phones, laptops, televisions) at least 1 hour before bedtime.

★ Devise a bedtime routine that includes wind-down activities such as reading a book or listening to music as well as essential bedtime preparations such as cleaning your teeth or washing your face.

★ Dim the lights in the evening.

★ Try not to work in bed (even in the daytime).

★ Get the temperature right – you might need extra blankets or an open window.

★ Don't lie in bed tossing and turning. If you can't sleep and you are still awake after 20 minutes, get up, stretch, read and try again when you feel sleepy.

★ Most importantly, if you have a bad night, don't worry, you *will* catch up.

MY TIME IS PRECIOUS

Setting boundaries is not about keeping people away, rather it is a powerful act of self-care.

Michelle Maros

SAYING *NO*

Saying *no* can be difficult. You may be anxious about upsetting others, fearful of rejection or of missing out on opportunities. But learning to say *no* is crucial to self-care. Remember, being a student comes with responsibility. You cannot meet the demands of higher education if you are frazzled and depleted. Learning to say *no* will ensure greater enjoyment of the things you say *yes* to.

It's tricky to back out if you've already agreed to something, so cultivate the habit of giving yourself breathing space before you say *yes*. Phrases like, "Can I get back to you?" or "I need to check my diary" are excellent ways of buying time to make a decision based on what you really want.

Remember, too, there are many ways to say *no*.
Why not try...

★ "I have another commitment."

★ "I won't be able to make it on this occasion."

★ "I'm going to pass this time."

★ "Maybe next time."

WE NEED TO DO A BETTER JOB OF PUTTING OURSELVES HIGHER ON OUR TO-DO LIST.

Michelle Obama

Connecting with your spirituality

Seeking meaningful connections to something outside of yourself is part of self-care. Attending to your spirituality is one way to do that, and one that does not have to involve commitment to a specific faith system. You can connect to your spirituality in a number of different ways. If you are a student with a faith, make your spiritual practices part of your weekly and daily plans.

Other ways to exercise your spirituality might include:

★ Nature

★ Creative arts

★ Friendships

★ Volunteering/campaigning

★ Meditation

Give it some thought.

EMAILS CAN WAIT

How often do you get to the end of the day feeling that you have been busy but not productive? Students often feel that to find focus they need to get the small jobs (like answering emails) out of the way, only to find that those little errands have a nasty habit of expanding to fill the whole day. It is tempting to think that you will only be able to concentrate on your coursework when you've done those small jobs. The truth is, there will always be little things to do. If you keep pushing back the big tasks, you will rarely get around to them.

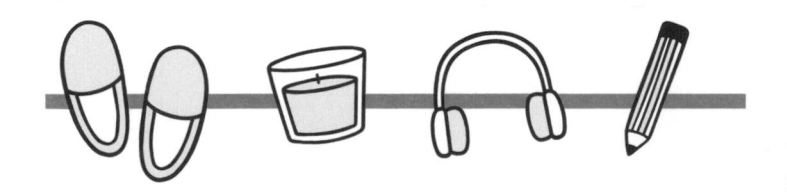

Try to shift your mindset on this. Put the projects that require your focus right up front. Those are the things that have the most impact on your well-being if they don't get done. Reassure yourself that the small jobs will fit in the space that is left over – and if they don't, chances are they were not that important to begin with and can be dealt with another day.

I EXERCISE
FOR

HEALTH,
ENERGY

AND
LOVE OF

MY BODY

EXERCISE

Being active is good for your motivation, energy and focus. As a student, you may find it difficult to exercise consistently and moderately. Try to move every day. It doesn't have to be a vigorous workout at the gym; some gentle yoga every other day is beneficial to how you feel and your ability to focus. A walk after lunch is an excellent habit to form and one that also puts a little structure into your day. If walking isn't possible for you, try stretching. Why not try dancing while you are waiting for your dinner to cook?

IN THE QUIET
MOMENTS, THE
DISCOVERIES
ARE MADE.

VERA FARMIGA

Solitude is where
I place my chaos to
rest and awaken my
inner peace.

Nikki Rowe

QUIET TIME

Student life can be frantic. It can be difficult even to think about self-care, never mind find time to do it. When planning your week, try to carve out a little time simply to be quiet. This could be sitting on a bench in the local park, treating yourself to a long soak in the bath or lying quietly in your room with your phone out of reach.

What does being quiet have to do with self-care? When you are still and not being distracted, that is the only time you can really hear what it is that you need. No social media influencers telling you what you should be thinking, eating, wearing or buying. No housemates, no family, no music, no phone. Just you. There's no pressure to empty your mind or focus on your breathing. Just be.

However you choose to spend your quiet time, listen to what your body and mind are telling you. Do you have aches or pains? Particular worries? Not only is this an act of self-care in and of itself, but it will help you to think about what further actions you might need to take.

KEEPING A JOURNAL

Writing might be the last thing you want to do after studying all day. But writing your thoughts and feelings out regularly can be a way to cut loose and is shown to support good mental health. Your journal is for you only, not for anyone else, so you can be honest and really let your feelings flow on the page. Best of all, where your journal is concerned, you don't need to reference, spellcheck, proofread or do a word count. It's a great way to finish your day.

WE ALL MAKE
MISTAKES,
AND IT'S NOT
UNTIL WE MAKE
MISTAKES THAT
WE LEARN.

Liam Hemsworth

MAKING MISTAKES

If you were an expert in your subject, you wouldn't need to be here, right? There are going to be occasions when you get things wrong. A lower grade than expected on your latest assignment; a concept you don't understand; a wrong answer in a seminar. When this happens (not if!), try not to panic. Everything is fixable.

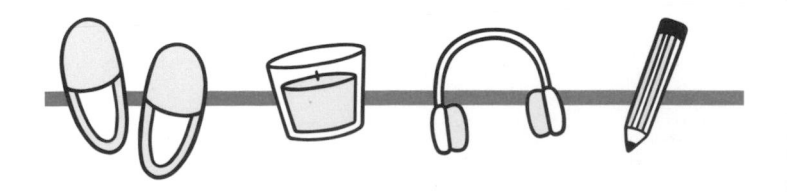

Be brave and look at your feedback. It's not the mistake that is the most important thing; it is how you deal with it and what you can learn from it that is important. Remember it was the work or the approach that wasn't right, not *you*. If you are concerned, ask for a meeting with the tutor – they may have office hours you can book. Give yourself time to do more research, practice questions or reading next time. Is there someone on the same course as you who can help? You might be able to help them with something in return. Sometimes you may need to do resits or resubmit the work. It's not ideal, but also not uncommon and nothing to be ashamed of. Be kind to yourself. Learning rarely happens in a straight line.

I ALLOW
MYSELF
TO MAKE
MISTAKES
AND I
GROW
AS A RESULT

PERFECTION
IS OFTEN THE
ENEMY OF
GREATNESS.

JANELLE MONÁE

PERFECTIONISM

Studies show that perfectionism is not intrinsically good or bad. Think of it as a spectrum or a scale, with healthy at one end and unhealthy at the other. Healthy perfectionism sounds like, "This project is so interesting! I really want to do a great job on this." It looks like finishing the day feeling satisfied and accomplished, taking breaks when you need them and being happy to work on other things. Healthy perfectionism is driven by ambition and joyful enthusiasm.

Unhealthy perfectionism sounds like, "If I screw up this project, it will be a disaster. I should pull an all-nighter." It looks like working until you're exhausted, ignoring other commitments, feeling guilty when resting and finishing the day feeling worried and unsatisfied. Unhealthy perfectionism is driven by fear of failure. The trouble is that unhealthy perfectionism involves standards that you can never attain, no matter how long you stay in the library!

If you slip into unhealthy perfectionism...

★ Acknowledge it

★ Break the work into smaller tasks, to give you a sense of accomplishment

★ Think how you might advise a friend who is overworking

★ Think about the process and not the outcome

★ Reconnect to what you love about studying

★ Remind yourself that your grades are not a reflection of your value as a person

★ Give yourself encouragement, not criticism

PROCRASTINATION

Ever noticed how the only time you feel like sorting out your sock drawer is when you have some work to hand in? Procrastination is very common among students. It might leave you with a sense of failure, or labelling yourself as "lazy" or "unproductive". But procrastination rarely has anything to do with laziness. More often than not it's fear. Students usually put things off because they feel overwhelmed and/or incapable. The irony of course is that the longer you leave it, the less time you have to do a good job. The only solution is action.

Choose the tiniest, easiest thing first. Anything to get you on the page. Plan your essay in bullet points. Print off the article. Draft an answer to the first question. Breaking the deadlock can feel difficult, so nurture yourself. Snacks, blankets, music, a warm drink, low lighting. Making it as pleasant an activity as possible will increase your chances of doing it.

You don't have to see the whole staircase, just take the first step.

Martin Luther King Jr

I APPROACH MY

TO-DO LIST

WITH

JOY, EASE

AND

ENTHUSIASM

WHEN THINGS GO WRONG

Being a student is just like any other time in your life, in the sense that sometimes things can go wrong. Life does not stop happening while you are at university or college. Events or circumstances can make it difficult for you to fully focus on your studies. It can sometimes be the case that studying itself can become a cause of great difficulty.

How do you take care of yourself when things aren't going right? Firstly, you must speak up. Tell someone. Struggling in silence is not good self-care. Talk to your personal tutor, your students' union, student service or guidance counsellors. They are on your side and are there to help you figure out what to do.

If your situation means that you can't concentrate on your work, don't try to force it. It's far better to take a day or two out (and perhaps request an extension) than to increase your anxiety by staring at a screen and getting nowhere. If this is you, you aren't the first student to be feeling this way – and you won't be the last.

HUMBLE PEOPLE ASK FOR HELP.

Joyce Meyer

DON'T GO IT ALONE

Asking for help need not be a big deal. Stuck with a difficult theory or concept? You won't be the only one! Ask around and see if anyone else is having trouble. Studying in pairs can be very effective if managed carefully. You could take it in turns to "teach" each other. This is a great way to consolidate your learning. Studying together reduces isolation, improves self-esteem and provides a sense of belonging.

SOMETIMES
GOOD THINGS
FALL APART SO
BETTER THINGS
CAN FALL
TOGETHER.

MARILYN MONROE

Asking for extensions

If circumstances are affecting your studies, request an extension. This could be a few days or a longer period of time. Valid reasons might include injury, being mentally or physically unwell, or an unexpected life event or crisis such as a bereavement. Most universities and colleges have rules around this. They may need evidence, or there may be a limit to how soon or how late you can make your request, so do check.

There is no shame in needing more time. If an extension is not possible, speak with your tutor anyway. There may be alternative ways they can help you, such as extra tuition or mentoring. The key thing here is not to wait until you are in crisis to talk to someone. Speaking up early is always the best approach.

I AM
CALM
AND
WELL
PREPARED

Trust yourself.
You know more than
you think you do.

Benjamin Spock

COPING WITH EXAM STRESS

There's no denying it: exams are stressful and unavoidable in most cases. How do you care for yourself during these times?

★ Eat well – now is not the time for junk food.

★ Get plenty of rest.

★ DO NOT CRAM! Plan your revision well in advance.

★ Get outside every day for light, fresh air and gentle exercise.

Remind yourself that although you want to do as well as possible, exams are not the be all and end all. You're going to be fine.

JUST BELIEVE IN YOURSELF. EVEN IF YOU DON'T, PRETEND THAT YOU DO AND AT SOME POINT YOU WILL.

Venus Williams

SWITCHING OFF

You probably spend a big chunk of your day looking at a screen as part of your daily studies as well as daily smartphone use. Screen fatigue can result in poor sleep, mood problems, anxiety and eye strain. Look after yourself by reading from hard copies occasionally, handwriting your notes and setting a screen cut-off time every day. You may find that these alternative methods help you to absorb information better. You might even enjoy the process of writing by hand.

IT IS

BENEFICIAL

FOR ME

TO TAKE
TIME

AWAY FROM

MY STUDIES

DOWNTIME IS PROCESSING TIME

There may come a time when you find yourself veering toward being a perfectionist, anxious about falling behind and even failing. You might be worrying that you only have one shot at this and you'd better seize the moment. Ideas like this may drive you to spend every spare moment engaged in study. You might feel guilty about taking any time off at all. If that sounds familiar, then you should know this: downtime is a critical part of studying.

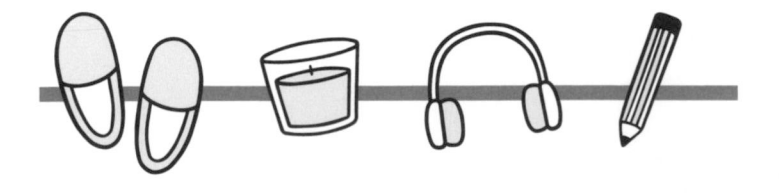

Learning happens in two parts: absorbing the information and processing it. Processing is your brain digesting, consolidating and storing the material. You cannot process while taking in new information.

Read that again. Your brain needs space to do this essential task of processing. Downtime is that space. Without it, the information may not stick. Build downtime into your weekly schedule, safe in the knowledge that while you are playing squash, reading trashy fiction, playing *Minecraft* or having a hot drink in the cafe on campus, your brain is ticking away in the background.

IF WE WAIT
FOR THE
MOMENT WHEN
ABSOLUTELY
EVERYTHING IS
READY, WE SHALL
NEVER BEGIN.

IVAN TURGENEV

Study nature, love nature, stay close to nature. It will never fail you.

Frank Lloyd Wright

I AM
SOOTHED,
SUPPORTED
AND
RENEWED
BY TIME
SPENT
OUTDOORS

IN TOUCH WITH NATURE

Being in green spaces is one of the best ways to take a break. Studies show that the benefits of time spent in nature include stress reduction, improved focus and enhanced creativity, as well as better sleep, memory, mood and a sense of connectedness. A park is good enough or simply take a route to campus that incorporates street trees. Perhaps you could recruit a friend to take a day trip with you on the train to the coast or out into the countryside. Taking yourself to a green space on a regular basis is a lovely way to care for yourself.

SOMETIMES
WHEN WE TAKE
A BREAK, WE
MAY FIND THAT
SOLUTIONS
THEN PRESENT
THEMSELVES.

Catherine Pulsifer

JUST BECAUSE
YOU TAKE
BREAKS DOESN'T
MEAN YOU'RE
BROKEN.

CURTIS TYRONE JONES

THE FUNDAMENTALS

You can't do everything perfectly all the time. Not studying, not relationships – not even self-care. Expecting yourself to implement everything you have read about self-care and studying is setting yourself up for failure. And you're not a failure; you're a human being, doing the best you can with what you have.

Setting the bar too high can be overwhelming and result in doing nothing at all, which can chip away at your confidence. But meeting the fundamentals on a regular basis will create an upward spiral, improving motivation and laying down a solid foundation on which you can build. Spend some time thinking about what the most important aspects of self-care are for you.

Write three sentences using one of the following structures:

"As long as I *brush my teeth/stretch* today,
I am doing alright."

"The most important thing for me today is
eating a proper breakfast/taking a walk."

_____

_____

_____

_____

_____

_____

I AM DOING

MY BEST

AND I AM

**GOOD
ENOUGH**

CONCLUSION

Your time in higher education is important and valuable – and so are you! Your studies should never come at the expense of self-care. In the end, unless you look after yourself, you may not achieve the success – or the grades – of which you are capable. Putting yourself first will help you make the most of university or college without it feeling like a battle and enable you to have fun along the way! You deserve that, you really do.

Take good care.

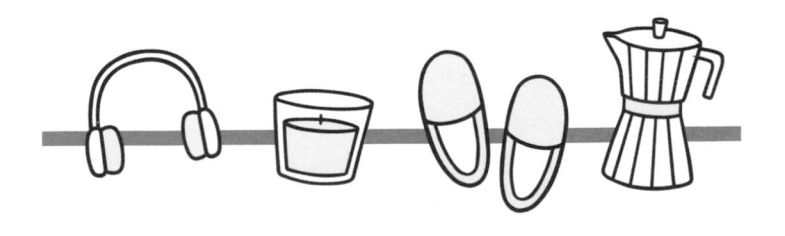

Student Hacks

Tips and Tricks to Make Uni Life Easier

Dan Marshall

ISBN: 978-1-78685-246-5

This manual covers everything from making your student loan stretch further and revision hacks to fitting more beer bottles in your fridge. Whether you're a fresh-faced fresher or a seasoned student searching for shortcuts, this trusty guide will make your uni life easier, more productive and more fun.

The Little Book of Student Food

Easy Recipes for Tasty, Healthy Eating on a Budget

Alastair Williams

ISBN: 978-1-78783-024-0

Every student needs to fill their belly as well as their brain. But even if you can barely make toast, this starter guide to killing it in the kitchen will give you what you need to succeed. From the very basics through to more adventurous dishes, these recipes are budget-friendly, super tasty and easy to make.

Have you enjoyed this book? If so, find us on Facebook at Summersdale Publishers, on Twitter at @Summersdale and on Instagram and TikTok at @summersdalebooks and get in touch. We'd love to hear from you!

www.summersdale.com